P.L. KLEIN

HATCHING TWITTER

The Ultimate Guide to Twitter Strategies for A Success Business, Learn All The Secrets From Top Twitter Users on How They Get All the Business Without Spending Anything!

Descrierea CIP a Bibliotecii Naţionale a României
P.L. KLEIN
   HATCHING TWITTER. The Ultimate Guide to Twitter
Strategies for A Success Business, Learn All The Secrets From
Top Twitter Users on How They Get All the Business Without
Spending Anything! / P.L. Klein. – Bucharest: Editura My Ebook,
2020
   ISBN 978-606-983-602-6

P.L. KLEIN

HATCHING TWITTER

**The Ultimate Guide to Twitter Strategies for
A Success Business, Learn All The Secrets From
Top Twitter Users on How They Get All the
Business Without Spending Anything!**

My Ebook Publishing House
Bucharest, 2020

TABLE OF CONTENTS

CHAPTER 1

INTRODUCTION

What Is Twitter, And Why Should You Be Interested In It?

Why indeed? Because, after all, isn't it just another social networking site?

I think it is a little more than that. It IS a way of networking with other people, that much is true, but you could also call it a phenomenon. Sharing knowledge, advice, updates and much more in just 140 characters is a challenge that thousands of new people are taking up every single day. Twitter has hit the headlines more and more in recent times, and revealing just a few of the stories that have been published should give you an idea of just how important this site can be to you.

When the Presidential race was on, both candidates were making good use of Twitter to garner support for their campaigns. Barack Obama is still the most followed person on the whole of Twitter... although he hasn't been tweeting much since he started running the country. He still has well over 600,000 followers at the last count however.

And celebrities are using the site more and more too – to connect with their fans, promote their careers and much more besides. Some of these have been proved to be fake, but there are plenty of real celebrity Twitterers out there too.

The British comedian, actor and writer Stephen Fry has the second biggest number of followers on the site. He often responds to messages and takes part in conversations as well. American actress Demi Moore proved that Twitter can be much more than just another social networking site by helping to prevent an apparent suicide bid by another user.

You can see how Twitter has pervaded the lives of many different people. You can make a difference with this site, and you can also use it for many different purposes, as we're about to find out in this book. But the main thing to remember at this stage is that you can reach a huge audience. It may not be anywhere near as big as the one President Obama enjoys, but you can still end up with thousands who will read every tweet you write.

Twitter is not just for the rich and famous – although judging by the number of stories along those lines that have been hitting the headlines recently, you may wonder.

But no matter what line of business you are in; whether you are based primarily online or you have offline interests as well, you CAN benefit from having a free account on Twitter. And this book will show you exactly how you can do it.

We'll explore everything you need to know during each section. You'll not only know how Twitter works and how to make the best of it, you'll also discover how you can make it work for YOU. There are certain points that you will need to bear in mind if you want to build up a huge band of followers instead of just having a few hundred, or even a few dozen. We'll cover all of these one by one.

We'll also cover the importance of getting set up in just the right way. Once you know what you are doing on Twitter, you will instantly be able to tell which people haven't taken the time to get set up properly. You won't be one of those because you will have read all the tips and techniques I am about to give you.

You'll soon see that the book is split up into several different sections. These have been designed to be read in that order, so as to get the best out of this book. You need to have a great home page before you start learning all about the tricks of the trade that I have included in Section Four.

So let's get started and go straight to Section One, so you can get started with the least of delay.

CHAPTER 2

WHAT TO DO ONCE YOU'VE JOINED

Okay, so you've gone to http://twitter.com and signed up for your free Twitter account. That is the easy bit, and it should only take a few moments to complete the process.

The first thing you need to think of when you sign up is what username you are going to use. This could depend on how long your own name is, as you only have a limited number of characters to use. Your username will then form part of your own unique home page address, i.e. http://twitter.com/username.

And of course you don't need to use your own name either. You could use your business name if you wish.

The next step is to go through the five step process I am about to share with you. Now I know you are probably itching to start 'tweeting' – the term that is given to sending messages through Twitter – but it is essential that you make sure you get your account sorted out properly first.

As you become more and more familiar with the site, you will be able to spot those people who have jumped in without completing all the steps I am going to show you. And there is one word for what their home pages look like – unprofessional. It can't be a coincidence that most of these people have either (a) tweeted a few times and then disappeared entirely, or (b) made sure all their messages are of a marketing kind.

There is nothing wrong with marketing on Twitter, but if you are going to heavily promote everything you have to sell, don't expect to get many followers or much success. You'll find out why as we go along. Incidentally all of these steps can be done by clicking on the 'settings' option at the top of your home page once you are logged in.

So let's get started with the first step, shall we?

Filling Out Your Bio (Profile)

Twitter is all about brevity. And when you only have 140 characters to use to create each new message, it shouldn't come as much of a surprise to find that your bio only consists of one line as well.

But it isn't much of a problem – provided you write it in the right way. You need to think about it from a certain angle to make sure you have a successful bio that draws people in. In other words, a good bio will get you more followers.

One good method to get ideas for your own bio is to have a look at what some other members have already done. Type a word into the search box – any word will do for the purpose of this example – and take a look at the results you get back. Click on a username and you will be taken into their home page, which will have their bio in the top right hand corner, underneath their little photo.

Which ones really get your attention? The best ones are generally those which describe the person and what they do without going into sales mode. Your bio is not the place for trying to sell people something. It is a place to introduce yourself, and nothing more.

You will no doubt also notice that some people don't bother to fill in their bios at all. This is a BIG no no. If your bio is not filled in, people only really have your tweets to go on to decide whether you will be worth following or not. And if they aren't interested in the latest few they read, you could easily lose a potential follower there.

So how do you write a great one line bio?

The trick is to think about what you do, and what you are on Twitter for. And above all, think in keywords. Remember that you haven't got much room to make an impression. Let's suppose you started off like this:

"Hi I am Dave and I'm from Texas in the US. I love internet marketing and..."

And at that point you probably have very few other characters left to make anything out of. More than half of the words in that piece are superfluous – 'am', 'and' and 'from', for example. It's not essential to tell everyone your name as your username will appear in the top right hand corner of the page anyway. And the same goes for your location, which you should fill in separately on your profile.

So let's go back to keywords. Remember that your Twitter home page can show up on Google's search pages, so you want to think about what pages you want to appear on. Twitter's own search facility can help people find you as well, so be sure to include all the relevant words you can.

The trick here is to get a balance between writing a proper sentence, and simply putting a string of keywords down. So an internet marketer who writes their own series of eBooks - as well as doing some affiliate marketing on the side – might come up with something like this:

"Internet and affiliate marketer; writer and promoter of eBooks."

You could go a bit longer than that, but for the purpose of the example do you see how effective a short phrase like that can be? It isn't a proper sentence as such, but it is packed with keywords and it manages to tell people 4 things that the person does.

So take time over your bio – it is a very important part of your home page. You'll be able to fill it in using the account tab in your settings.

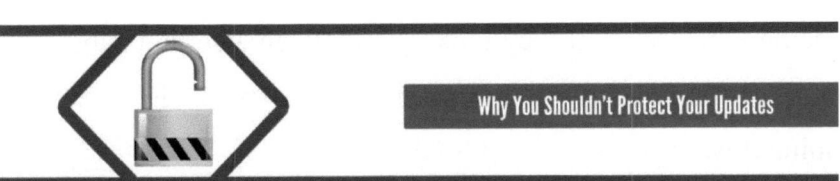

Why You Shouldn't Protect Your Updates

Why You Shouldn't Protect Your Updates

I just want to mention this because if you are going to use Twitter to help promote your business, you shouldn't protect your updates.

An update is basically a message that you post to your home page. If you protect it (which can be done by ticking the appropriate box on your profile page), it means no one who visits your home page will be able to see your updates... unless you accept them as a follower.

So basically they have to send you a message asking if they can see them, and if you say yes, they will be able to. What a crazy way of doing things! This is really only suitable for people who want to Twitter with friends and family. It's great under those circumstances, but it's not so good if you are trying to use Twitter to enhance your business and promotional efforts.

The other point to bear in mind is that if they can't see what you are tweeting about, all they have to go on is your one line bio. That's pretty much it. You are preventing people from seeing your tweets if they look up tweets on a certain subject as well, so you won't get anywhere near as many followers by doing this.

The bottom line is, make sure you don't protect your updates.

Uploading Your Picture(s)

Once you've filled out your bio, it's time to sort your picture out. You have three main choices to go for here:

- You can use a real photo of yourself
- You can use a character or cartoon picture of yourself
- You can use a logo or other picture that is relevant to your business

The fourth option – which I haven't listed above as I feel very strongly against it – is to leave the default picture in place. This looks like two zeroes separated by a line. In short, it is called a default picture for a reason; it's up to you to change it!

Some people think that only a real photo is good enough on Twitter, if you want to be taken seriously. I disagree. There are some terrific people on Twitter who quite rightly use their business logo, or perhaps the logo of their main website or blog. Character or cartoon pictures can also work very well in some

17

cases; presumably cartoonists wouldn't dream of choosing anything else.

In short, choose what you feel comfortable with. The two main rules are to make sure you replace that default image with something better, and to ensure that it is clear and of good quality.

Designing Your Profile Page

Designing Your Page

Look for the design tab in your settings section. At the time of writing you have a dozen themes to choose. These are basically your backgrounds.

But you can also upload your own background if you wish – and this is by far the best choice to make. It will enable you to stand out as an individual, as no one else will have the same one.

There are sites which provide templates for you to change and alter as you see fit, or you can design something yourself. Some Twitter users have even created backgrounds for other people on the site! You will notice that some have made sure their website address and additional marketing information is included within the background... which is the primary reason why you should think about doing this yourself.

There are some points you should be aware of here though. The most important one is to be aware of the limitations that are in place. Take a look at your home page for a moment and you will see what I mean. The main section of your home page – the bit with all the tweets and your information on it – is enclosed in a specific portion of the page, in the center.

This means your background design essentially wraps around it. So if you opt for a central design, you aren't going to see it. Instead, think of creating two columns – one either side of the central part of the page. You may need to experiment with the dimensions as well, to make sure your design can easily be seen by other people when they visit your page.

Surf around Twitter for a while and have a look at some other home pages whose owners have tried to do this. You can see what happens if the dimensions are wrong; you might only be able to see the first half of someone's email address or website address. Needless to say that doesn't help when it comes to enabling people to get in touch with you!

This all depends on the resolution of your monitor – and of the monitors of everyone who views your home page. But you can tweak what you make to ensure that everyone can see it properly.

Start Tweeting!

Okay, so if you've completed all the above steps you should now have a home page which looks pretty good. All that remains now is to start tweeting, so you have some worthwhile content on it to attract the attention of anyone who finds your page.

Most of the time, the first tweet anyone makes is something along the lines of 'figuring out how to use Twitter'! Don't feel you have to stick to this however – it's become a little boring in many cases. Take the opportunity to tell people what you are going to be tweeting about in the future. Bear in mind that it is going to take a while to build up a backlog of tweets for people to read, so you need to try and make sure you give them something to look forward to.

Our fictitious internet marketer could start something like this:

"Building my brand new affiliate website – details soon!"

"Made $357 in affiliate sales today – will share more info in future tweets."

Do you see how these make people want to read more? They also contain good keywords – and we will explore how to make sure you can benefit from those in a later section.

The key is really to remember why you joined Twitter in the first place. Don't just tweet about anything and everything – make sure you stay on topic as much as you can. If your reason for joining was to share your knowledge about internet marketing in the hope of selling some eBooks about that subject, bear that in mind at all times. You want to create traffic to your website or blog as well, no doubt. So think about the type of people who will enjoy your site and work at getting their attention.

In short, you should always think before you tweet. Don't post messages just for the sake of it; some users post dozens every day, and that can be a bit overwhelming. I remember following one person once who looked like they could be worth keeping in touch with... but within a couple of days I got overwhelmed by the sheer volume of messages they were sending.

Needless to say I ended up un-following them just as fast!

You don't need to post every day if you don't want to or can't manage it. A lot of people post first thing in the morning or whenever they sit down at their computer to start work. You will probably fall into a pattern of your own as you settle into the familiarity of having a Twitter account.

One final tip before we close this section of the book; take a look at your one line bio before you tweet each time, at least to begin with. It is a good way of keeping yourself on track to post worthwhile tweets that people will find interesting.

CHAPTER 3

UNDERSTANDING YOUR HOME PAGE

If you have followed through on all the steps I showed you in the first section of this book, you should now have a pretty impressive home page to look at.

While I am sure you probably have plenty of ideas for some more tweets to post, now would be a good time to take a closer look at your home page to understand what the various parts can tell you.

Underneath your username, you will have your location and bio. You will also be able to see a link to your website or blog. And underneath that you will notice there are three things listed one after the other. Each one has a number underneath it that you can click on too. Let's look at these in a bit more depth.

The Concept of Following

These are all the people you are following on Twitter. If you click on that number you will get a complete list of them to view. You can click on this number on other people's home pages too – which is a big clue to how you can find lots of relevant people to follow!

What Are Followers?

These are all the people who are following you. Once again, clicking on the number brings up a list of them all. You can review this from time to time to see whether anyone is following you that you are not following in return. You don't have to follow everyone… but reciprocity is a nice thing.

Twitter Updates

'Updates' basically refers to how many tweets you have posted on your Twitter account. Every new message you write and publish will push this figure up by one.

Some people celebrate milestones as they reach them. You might occasionally see someone announcing their 100th or even 1000th tweet and beyond. If you do this, it's a nice idea to thank your followers for inspiring you to keep tweeting!

If you click on this figure, it will take you into a page which lists all your own tweets. And of course, anyone else visiting your home page will be able to see these too.

Your @Username

This used to be the 'replies' tab, but the team at Twitter have changed it so you can now see every single tweet on the site which has your username in it.

This is actually more beneficial because there may be occasions when people do not actually reply to you, but they do mention you in one of their own tweets. You can see whether you are making a name for yourself or not.

But the main reason to be interested in this tab is because Twitter users can reply to tweets that other users have made. Let's say for example that you went ahead and published the tweet which said "Made $357 in affiliate sales today – will share more info in future tweets."

Someone may have read that and been very interested in what you had to say. So they look to the right hand side of your message and see two things – a star symbol (which lets them favorite that tweet if they wish) and a curved arrow symbol, which if they click on it will let them reply to you.

Their reply will appear on their home page and in their own timeline, and it will still be visible to be read by everyone else. But it will also appear in your @username tab, which is why it is worthwhile to check this page every now and then to see whether anyone has any questions for you. Engaging in conversation with other users is one sure way to build up more followers as well, as we will find out later on.

And let's face it, if you aren't going to interact with anyone on a regular basis, you won't achieve the results you are looking for.

Direct Messages

This is a neat feature of Twitter that allows you some security and privacy, should you need it.

Basically there may be times when you want to ask another member something that you don't want the world as a whole to see. The best example of this is if you were looking for someone to provide a service.

Let's say you wanted to find a designer to create that unique background for your Twitter home page. You may have started following a few people who could possibly provide that service for you. In this case you might want to send a direct message to one of them, asking if they could do it and if so, how much for.

They can then reply directly back to you in the same manner. This would mean you could actually exchange email addresses without letting the whole of Twitter know what they are! This is quite a common practice, so it's good to know what direct messages are there for.

And once again, make sure you check your messages from time to time, just as you check your @username tab. Incidentally on your settings page under the notices tab, you can elect to receive emails whenever someone starts following you, or sends you a direct message. I recommend you tick this, unless your followers start coming in lorry loads at a time. It means that you are less likely to miss any important DMs, as direct messages are often referred to.

It is also a nice gesture to send someone a direct message if they have started following you. This is easy if you get a steady stream of followers. But if they start arriving en masse you may need to try out a third party (and usually free) software solution that allows you to send direct messages to a number of people at once.

For my money, auto DMing is less preferable to the personal touch however.

Favorites Explanation

One of the great things about Twitter is the number of resources you can glean from it. A good example of this are links to other websites which may prove useful.

Writers often post links to websites and blogs they think other writers will like. Internet marketers do the same for their comrades. So do moms, freelancers, self employed people, businessmen… and so on. Everyone you can think of has interests and most of the dedicated users on Twitter actually like to share them.

But of course once you start following a lot of people and your own tweets start appearing in the public timeline as well, it can be very difficult to keep track of the tweets you like.

That's why we have favorites. Remember a while back I mentioned those two symbols you will see next to every single tweet posted by another person? There is the arrow for responding directly to a tweet, and there is a star. If you click on that star it will turn yellow, and it will also go onto your favorites' page. So the next time you need to refer to that particular tweet, or you want to retrieve that web address, you can go to your favorites page to do it.

It's much easier than going through all your old tweets to find it!

CHAPTER 4

USING TWITTER FOR MARKETING PURPOSES

Now you should be all set to start using Twitter in the way you REALLY want to use it. There are thousands of people who are already well aware of how responsive this site can be, and also how much it can help you to build up a steady stream of traffic to your desired website or business.

In this section we are going to cover the most important points when it comes to marketing on Twitter. There is a right way and a wrong way to do this, and if you go at it in a heavy promotional way, you aren't going to get the results you want. I have come across users in the past who have clearly set up lots of separate Twitter accounts and have just one thing to promote. And strangely enough, they never hang around long enough to learn how to do it properly.

So let's see what you need to do to make sure you get it right first time.

The First Rule Of Marketing

The First Rule of Marketing

This is the one that confuses a lot of people. That's because it is a contradiction in terms. You see, the first rule of marketing is not to do it all the time!

Now I know what you might be thinking. You wanted to start using Twitter because you heard about other people who were doing the same thing. And they were getting more sales, more visitors to their websites, more contacts... the whole caboodle.

Now how on earth are you going to get all that if you aren't going to do any marketing?

That is where the distinction is. You ARE going to do some marketing... but you aren't going to do it all the time. A good way of understanding how this works is to think about how you like to use the site yourself. Do you like to go on Twitter to read nothing but marketing messages from other people? Of course you don't. You like to go on the site to find likeminded people that are worth following. You want to get some benefits from being on there, and you aren't going to get those benefits if the only people you follow are people who are constantly promoting their own stuff all the time. If you wanted to read a slew of sales pages you could go straight on the internet to do it.

So when it comes to attracting the attention of other people you need to think along those same lines. Ask yourself what your followers are looking to get from you. The answers to this question will come from your reasons for being on the site in the first place. So if you are a writer and you are looking to link up with other writers (and you have a writing blog you want to get them to visit), you need to think about what they want from you. Knowledge and advice are two hot favorites, whatever subject you and your followers (and future followers) are interested in.

What you need to do is become known as someone who gives good advice and also offers good links to external websites other than your own. It's very much the same as giving away freebies to establish a bond of trust between you and your followers. If you give them a website address that has nothing to do with you (and isn't even an affiliate link), and they like it, they will realize that you are someone worth following. They know you aren't just trying to sell them stuff all the time.

That means that when you do direct them to your website or blog – generally for a very good reason – they are much more likely to follow that link to see what you have got for them.

Some people only post a tweet when they have updated their blog and have a new post for everyone to read. But while this doesn't always mean that the person is trying to sell something, it can lead to apathy on the part of the people who are following that person. It's much better to throw in a link to a fresh post on your blog perhaps every four or five tweets, or maybe more. This isn't a mathematical formula, but you can see that separating out yourself serving links with others than are purely for the benefit of your followers, is well worth doing.

This more subtle way of marketing is not only more rewarding in the long term, it is also more enjoyable for you. It will force you to become more engaged with other people on the site – and that is an excellent way to draw people in.

Who Are You Marketing To?

We have covered this to a degree already, but since we are now into the marketing section of this book it is worth covering it in more depth.

You need to figure out the primary 'ideal' person whose attention you really want to grab on Twitter. Not every follower has to fit this model, but you should make sure that the vast majority of them do. For example, a website designer may want to attract the attention of people who are looking for someone to design their website. Writers will be looking for people who may want them to write something. And people who work successfully from home may want to attract the attention of other people who want to be able to do the same thing.

The first two examples show people who want to sell services. The final example shows someone who could be selling either a product or a service, or both. But in both cases the person knows who they want to reach and why they want to reach them. That knowledge will influence the type of messages they will tweet for their followers.

The point I am making here is that having a huge number of followers is not the only thing you should be aiming for. Let's say you have ten thousand people following you on Twitter. Now that is a huge number and something to be proud of. Let's also say that you are an affiliate marketer and you ultimately want to introduce people to your range of eBooks and other items you are hoping to sell.

How well do you think you would do if your ten thousand followers encompassed all kinds of people in all walks of life? Most of them might have full time jobs, other interests or be interested in anything other than affiliate marketing. I'm sure you would agree that your results would be anything but spectacular.

Now let's consider the picture again if you could build up that same following. The only difference this time is that most of those followers have some kind of interest in affiliate marketing. They may be affiliate marketers themselves. They may have an interest in affiliate marketing and want to find out how they can earn lots of money doing what you do.

Do you see the difference?

Your followers must match up (by and large) to your purpose for being on Twitter. It's obvious that anyone and everyone can choose to follow you if they wish. But the content of your tweets should be enough to make sure that the majority of people who follow you share the same interest that you do.

The ideal thing in this example would be to make sure the vast majority of your tweets would be about affiliate marketing, or some aspect of it. You could branch out into other similar areas if you wish, but it might be worth exploring affiliate marketing in depth so you have plenty of ideas for worthwhile tweets.

It can be a good idea to make a list of topics or subjects that you can use for this purpose. And don't be afraid to ask questions or split a topic into a number of related tweets if you wish. As you become more familiar with Twitter you will see that people have created a number of different ways that you can connect with people by sending worthwhile tweets on the site.

Incidentally, asking questions is a good way to start conversations with people. You will find that giving out web links to useful sites, or tweeting about good topics will encourage replies anyway. But asking questions invites people to reply. It may not happen all the time, but on other occasions you may find yourself inundated! It all allows you to experiment with the site though, and if you ask the right questions you might even end up getting ideas for other affiliate products to promote, in this example.

If it helps, write down a short description of the audience you are trying to attract and tack it up above your computer. This will help you keep on track as far as your tweeting is concerned.

How To Find People To Follow

How To Find People To Follow

Let's talk a little bit now about following other people. One of the easiest ways to get people to follow you is to start following them first.

Makes sense, doesn't it? But as we found out above, you need to find the right people, and this rule applies as much to following people as it does to making sure the right ones follow you. So let's see how we can make sure you find the right people to follow from the start.

Let me point out here that the worst thing you can do is to sit back and wait for people to start following you. Some people can make this work, but it takes a concerted effort and many people just don't have the time to start like this. The easiest way to start is for you to get pro- active and to start following them first.

So… how do you find them?

Well, there are several ways and the first one begins with Twitter itself. If you take a fresh look at your home page and scroll right down to the bottom of the page, you will see a link in that bar across the bottom. It says 'search'. That's the one you need to click on.

You may also have noticed that there is a link at the top of the page; this one says 'find people'. You might think that is the best one to use, but that means you need to search for a specific name. It's good if you have some colleagues you want to find, because all you need to do is key in their name and any relevant Twitter accounts will pop up. You can then add them to the people you are following.

But we are focusing on searching for people you don't yet know. And to do this, we go back to the wonderful world of keywords.

So, once you have clicked on the search link you will be taken to the main Twitter search page. It looks a little like any other search engine, and as such you simply need to type in who you are looking for. Not names though – you are looking more accurately for what people DO, or what they are interested in.

We'll continue with the example on affiliate marketing we introduced above, so we can see how this works and how to get the best from it. If you type affiliate marketing into the box and search for appropriate results, you will get a slew of results coming back at you. These will have the most recent tweets first, which is good because if someone used to tweet about the topic regularly but isn't interested in it any more, those tweets will be way down the list.

You will see from the way the results are displayed that the name of the person who wrote the message comes first. You can then read the actual message, which will have the words or phrase you searched for in bold letters. It's worth remembering here that the search facility on Twitter works in exactly the same way as it does on any search engine. So if you want to search for the words affiliate marketing in any order, or with one appearing without the other, simply type them in as they are.

If on the other hand you want to search for them exactly as they are above, make sure you type them in quote marks, like this: "affiliate marketing". This will enable you to get a list of tweets which only feature that exact phrase. In this case it doesn't matter much either way, but it can be worth bearing in mind in some situations.

What you will generally find when it comes to scanning the results page is that some of the tweets will be more interesting than others. This can alert you to other members which could be worth following. If you see anyone who really catches your attention, click on the username to find out more about them. You can also click on the picture if you want to – it will still take you to their home page.

If you read their bio and a few more of their tweets and you think they are going to be worth following on a regular basis, here's what you do. Underneath their picture you will see a gray shaded button with the word 'follow' in it. Click on it and wait for the response. It should change to show the word 'following' and feature a small green tick as well. Just for good measure you will also get a tan line underneath that with a message telling you that you are now following that particular person.

One good point worth noting – whenever you find someone in the results that you might want to follow, use the middle key of your mouse to click through to their home page. It means you will get a new page opening up, and you won't lose your results page.

The next part of the process is basically to repeat the above process again. Carry on going through the list of results and find people who fit the description of your ideal follower. Who do you want to be introducing your business to, whatever that business might be? Find them and follow them!

Another point to remember is not to limit yourself to one keyword. So in this example you might end up searching for the phrase affiliate product as well. You can also look for other derivatives and similar phrases that people might tweet about if they are talking about affiliate marketing. Make a list and check them all in turn.

You will also see that because Twitter gives you real time results, the page will update to tell you how many new tweets have been published since you performed your search. All you need to do is press F5 and refresh to add those to the ones you have got already.

This process does take some time, but it is well worth doing. You can probably add several dozen followers in an evening, if not more. And once you have done that, be prepared to start adding followers yourself!

You see, the act of reciprocity comes into play here. Most of the people who you start following will follow you back. Not all of them do, but most should. And that means you are starting to build your network on Twitter – quickly and easily.

And once you have used this initial technique to get your foot on the ladder that is Twitter, there is another one you can use too. If you remember, you can check the list of people you are following by clicking on your 'following' figure on your home page.

Click on that now and I will reveal another good way to find people to follow. Incidentally once you have a few people following you, you can do this with that set of figures as well.

Let's use our ongoing example again here. You are into affiliate marketing. And so are a lot of the people you are following. So it stands to reason that those people are going to be following other similar people as well.

The idea here is to find other suitable people by looking at the networks of other people. All you do is hover your mouse over each username in the list. You will notice that if they have filled their bio in, it will appear as you hover your mouse.

Another good reason why you should have your own one filled in, as it will help more people to find and follow you!

So, click on a name that looks promising, and then when you reach their home page make sure you click on their 'following' tab. You now need to go through that list of people to see whether there is anyone that you would like to follow yourself. You can do the same with the 'followers' tab as well.

Do you see how easy it can be to find like minded people on a site with as many members as Twitter has? I'm sure you can. These methods do take time but they are very rewarding. And the more people you get in your network, the more people seem to be able to find you. Because there are a lot of people on Twitter who use the same techniques as I have just shared with you. That means you yourself will be much easier to find as you start showing up on other people's home pages and followers lists.

Of course, another reason why more people will follow you is if you give great value with your tweets. Do you remember the importance of making sure that you don't always promote your own interests? The more you can look after your followers, the more you will be rewarded as a result.

And that is the next point on our journey into understanding and benefiting from Twitter.

How To Make Sure You Don't Lose Followers

Twitter allows you to un-follow people as well as follow them. That means if you start following someone and then change your mind for some reason, you can choose not to follow them anymore.

But of course, this means that other people can un-follow you too! So how do you make sure that doesn't happen?

Well, it's all about giving people quality tweets and good advice. Think along the lines of developing your network and forming connections with people rather than simply trying to sell stuff to them. People can tell if your only reason for using Twitter is to promote your own business.

But that isn't the only reason you could lose followers. The key to a good tweet is held in the phrase above – quality tweets and good advice. You don't have to pack good advice into every single tweet, but they should all be of good quality. By all means say hi or good morning when you write your first tweet

45

of the day, but make a point of making more of it than that. What else could you write about to enhance it?

Similarly unless you are using Twitter for non-business purposes, don't start telling everyone what you are eating, or how much coffee you have just drunk. You need to ask yourself each time, BEFORE you publish your tweet, whether or not your followers are going to be interested enough to read it.

Some people might stop following you if you show no signs whatsoever of interacting with your followers. Now you don't need to start talking to every single individual and messaging them every hour of the day – particularly if you have thousands of followers – but it IS good to interact wherever you have a reason to.

For example, if I see someone has posted a worthwhile link to a useful website, I will reply to them and thank them for it. It's good to tell them why you liked it as well. It can get a dialog going and it shows you are interested in what your followers have to say, and not just in what you are saying yourself.

But the main thing to remember above all else is not to offend people. Some people like to be controversial, but it is rarely a good idea to be offensive in any form if you want to create a loyal and interested following. One misplaced tweet could be all it takes to lose the followers you have worked so hard to build.

In short, if your tweets are always well thought out; if they are always of good quality; and if they always give good value and are worth reading, you shouldn't get too many people unfollowing you at all.

Oh, and one other thing – make sure you shorten your URLs as well. There is nothing worse than treating people to a huge great long URL. And it may not even be seen properly anyway. Use TinyURL to shorten all your URLs so they take up less space. This is one of the most common ways to do so on Twitter.

CHAPTER 5

TRICKS OF THE TRADE

Think of this section as being your advanced level education on Twitter! Once you start using the site on a regular basis it does help to become familiar with a few of the finer points of using it, since it will help you to get the best out of it in the process.

So let's focus on each one in turn and see what they have to offer us.

How Do #Hashtags Work?

These provide you with a way to track tweets – both yours and those written by other people. In fact if you take a look at your list of trending topics on your home page, you will sometimes see a word preceded by a hashtag - # - in that section.

So how exactly do you go about using them?

Well, it's easy. Let's say you are a writer and you are interested in taking part in the National Novel Writing Month. This goes by the quirky shortened name of NaNoWriMo.

So what you might do, if you want to attract the attention of other interested writers when you tweet about this, is to include the hashtag #NaNoWriMo after each relevant tweet you make. You can also track other tweets by typing that hashtagged phrase - #NaNoWriMo – into the search box on Twitter. If you do this you will see that the results show up all tweets that have that hashtag included in them.

Now you might think that hashtags aren't actually that important. After all, we already know that we can search for keywords, so why bother with a hashtag? It's really only a keyword with a hash symbol in front of it, isn't it?

Well... yes and no. Hashtags are now useful mostly because people can use them to indicate shortened tags that people wouldn't look up as keywords. This is particularly the case when a long term is shortened drastically to make it fit on Twitter. For example, #WSUVJS stands for the WSU Virtual Journalism Summit. If someone reads one of your tweets regarding the subject and sees that hashtag, they know they can search for that tag and find other tweets on the same subject. Finding them all otherwise could be a nightmare.

You don't always have to use hashtags, but it's good to know they are there. And as we have seen, they can help you with both categorizing your own tweets and finding other people's too.

Keywords And The Benefits Of Them

Yes we're back to keywords again. If you are really serious about trying to attract a specific group of people on Twitter, you should make the effort to become familiar with the keywords they are likely to be looking for.

We know that keywords can help people to find our tweets – and our bio – on Twitter. But if you can do some research and find more keywords as a result, you should find that you get even better results.

There are plenty of keyword tools online that can be used for free, and you should be able to produce some kind of list that can help you target the right kind of people.

Keep an eye on the tweets that get a good response as well. Sometimes you will get responses from your followers even if you don't ask for them. You might get replies or direct messages, but they will both point to a tweet that has been popular or got a lot of attention for some reason.

The more familiar you become with the site and the more you learn about what your followers want, the more accurate you can be in attracting more people.

Now you might be thinking that we have overdosed on keywords somewhat. But that simply isn't true. I can't tell you how important they are. Think about what happens as you become more and more established on Twitter. You might get 100 followers in your first week, so that's 100 home pages (plus your own) that your tweets will show up on. Don't forget that if you look at your own home page, you can see all the tweets published by everyone you are following. That means your own will show up on all your followers pages as well.

And of course, as you are clicking on other people's lists of followers to add more to your own list, so other people are clicking on other lists as well. And the more lists your own Twitter username shows up on, the more followers you are likely to get.

In other words, the more places you show up in on the site, the better your results are likely to be.

Advertising Your Twitter Status Elsewhere To Get More Followers

Do you feel as if you still don't have enough in the way of followers? No problem. So far we have only focused on getting followers on Twitter itself. But of course you can find people and encourage them to follow you in lots of other places as well.

The easiest way to do this would be to add a note to your blog telling people they can find you on Twitter. But why write something when you can display a badge instead?

Twitter is very helpful in this respect. It has a page dedicated to providing badges for you to use free of charge, although it isn't the easiest page to find. It's located at http://twitter.com/badges. As you can see, they have some badges that are designed for specific sites, chiefly other social networking sites. But if you want one for your blog or website, or any other site you might be a member of, click on the 'other' option and click on continue to carry on.

As you'll see you can either go for a plain html widget, which does actually look quite nice, or you can go all out for the

Flash version. Just select your choice and continue once again. It's then a question of copying and pasting the code into your website.

You'll be interested to know that Twitter isn't the only source of badges for promoting your Twitter account elsewhere either. If you scroll to the bottom of any Twitter page you will see a link to the 'apps' section. From here you can explore countless widgets and other items that have been created by fans. And of course there are other websites online that have their own Twitter badges and widgets they will give you the code for.

The important thing is not to overdo it. There is no need to put a huge Twitter 'follow me!' sign in neon on every single page of your blog, for example. But you should make a list of all the sites and blogs that you have or you are a member of. Then you can gradually work your way around them and install some kind of widget on each one.

The great thing about these is that they update as well. When you install your widget it will usually have around the last half a dozen tweets on it. But as you update your account and post more tweets, you will find that your badges and widgets will also update automatically.

You can also opt to have a simple banner on your site if you wish. These often have some kind of bird picture based on the one on the Twitter website. People are then invited to click on it and follow you on Twitter if they wish. You might want to use a combination of these to see which ones work best for you.

Another way to connect with people is to write articles that would appeal to the kind of followers you want to attract. You can distribute these to article directories, post them on your blog, or write them for other blogs if you can. At the end you simply say that you tweet about your chosen subject on Twitter, and then include your home page address so people can find you.

It couldn't be easier to build up a significant Twitter following, could it?

CHAPTER 6

ESTABLISHING A PRESENCE ON TWITTER, AND WHY IT PAYS OFF (CONCLUSION)

So we have taken a journey through the website that is Twitter, and we have seen how to use it in the best possible way. We have also learned how to attract the right kind of followers, and how to make the best of our Twitter account so we can enhance the success of our business as well.

The most successful people on Twitter who have their followers hanging on every word will all tell you that they didn't get to that position overnight. This is an important fact to remember when you are at the beginning of setting up your Twitter account. It doesn't take too long to get a few hundred followers, to be sure, but if you want to get something in the region of ten thousand and above, as some people have, brace yourself for some work.

Of course I say 'work', but I don't mean hard work. This is enjoyable remember, and it can reward you in many more ways than you might think. Being an active member of Twitter (with the emphasis on the word 'active') makes you more visible. It makes you easier to find and easier to connect with too.

Many people focus on using it just to try and make more money. There is nothing wrong with trying to increase your business revenues as a result of using Twitter, but this shouldn't be your initial concern. The rewards don't always come as a direct result of promoting something in a tweet and then getting a sale from that tweet. You need to think further afield too.

I have known people who have had other users contact them to see if they would be interested in doing some work for them. Writers have bagged clients from Twitter, web designers have had people ask them if they could do work for them, and countless other people no doubt have similar stories they could tell.

Twitter is all about MAKING CONNECTIONS. Ultimately it is about making contact with other people who have similar interests to yours. That is why you need to regularly post tweets that have nothing to do with making sales. Unfortunately some newbies to Twitter simply don't get this. Twitter has rules and regulations just as every site does, and if every single tweet you make is about selling something, you are likely to meet with a temporary (or even permanent) ban on your account.

But as we have seen in the pages of this book, why go in for hard and fast promotion all the time when the softly, softly approach works so much better? If you aren't convinced now of the sheer amount of value you can get from Twitter, and the site can get from you, then I suggest you read through this book again!

Twitter does reward those people who use it the way it is supposed to be used. I have made some good contacts through the site that I never would have had if I hadn't taken the time to establish myself on there. Most of the people who use the site know enough to steer clear of anyone who has the default background, no picture and only one or two promotional tweets. These people usually have lots of people they are following... and very few if any people following them back.

For some reason these people assume that they can use Twitter to spam people with messages that are self serving and don't hold any value. At least the soon abandoned accounts seem to point to the fact that they get the picture pretty quickly.

No matter whether you are starting out with a new business, or you are looking for a new way to reach more customers and get hold of new ones, Twitter can be just what you are looking for. Don't underestimate the power of it; you will get back far more than you put in – provided you do invest in it.

People have found jobs through Twitter. Others have expanded their own business. Still more have found a site which allows them to express themselves and directly get in touch with people. While it is quite neat to be able to send a message to a movie star or musician, it's far better and more rewarding to strike up a conversation with someone who is a real authority in your line of work.

Perhaps that is the best piece of advice I could give you, ultimately, when it comes to understanding Twitter. Some people 'don't get it'. They can't understand why you would want to tweet short messages of 140 characters or less. Why tell people what you are doing?

The best way to use the site is to think laterally and imaginatively. Twitter actually makes it easy to communicate with thousands of people, thanks to the 140 character limit. They have actually made your work far easier! Even on my busiest days when I have plenty of work to do, I can still find a few seconds to post a good resource to my Twitter account. I can still find time to connect with my followers – purely because this microblogging tool is a lot faster to use than a standard blog.

The very essence of Twitter that some people find pointless is what makes it work so well. The people who understand this are the people who have the most followers on the site. They have the most active accounts, and take part in the largest number of conversations.

YOU can become one of them. I can tell you all about the benefits of this site, but it is up to you to make the most of them. Yes it does require some work, but the rewards are far in excess of the work you will need to put in. Once you try it and see that it's true, you shouldn't have any trouble making the most of your brand new Twitter account!

Utilize all of these strategies and keep an eye on the major players in your niche and market, emulate their strategies and make notes on the things that create the most buzz.

Implement different strategies in your business on Twitter and don't be afraid to do some trial and error.

So what are you waiting for? It's time to make a name for yourself out there on Twitter.

9 786069 836217

Printed by Libri Plureos GmbH in Hamburg, Germany